5-a-day World - T
Gary Goos

Written & Illustrated by
Jess Porter

This is a story about Gary Gooseberry and how he learned that friends are always there, when you need them……

Gary Gooseberry was often a naughty little YumYum.

He was always getting into trouble with his teachers and he would often fight with the other YumYums at break and lunch time.

One day, he was being silly with his football and kicked it right at Terry Turnip.

Poor Terry Turnip was hurt quite badly and was very upset.

Gary Gooseberry was sent to head teacher Connie Cauliflower's office, where he had to sit on the naughty carpet for one hour.

That one hour seemed to last forever.

There was nothing to do except watch the clock going…

tick…tock…tick…tock…tick…tock…

Gary Gooseberry was so bored, he nearly fell asleep.

Eventually, the hour was up and Gary Gooseberry could leave.

As he left head teacher Connie Cauliflower's office, the school bell rang and it was time to go home.

Gary Gooseberry lived near Bramble Valley in a medium sized house.

It was not very colourful and needed a lot of work doing on it.

Mr. Gooseberry was in the Army and had been away from home for a very long time.

Mrs. Gooseberry was too busy looking after all the children to look after the house as well, so the house began to look ruined.

Gary Gooseberry had six sisters and nine brothers.

When Gary Gooseberry arrived home, he began to fight with his brothers.

One of his brothers told their mum that Gary Gooseberry had been very naughty at school and had been sent to the head teacher's office.

Mrs. Gooseberry was very cross with Gary Gooseberry and sent him to his bedroom.

Whilst he was sat in there all alone, he had time to think about just how naughty he had been…

'I know!' he said. 'I will make it up to my mum by fixing the house, whilst dad is away.'

Gary Gooseberry sneaked out of his bedroom and went to call on his friends to ask for their help.

First he went to Adam Artichoke's house.

'Hello! Please can you help with a special surprise for my mum?' asked Gary Gooseberry.

'Yes I will, but only if you promise to always be nice to me.' said Adam Artichoke.

Gary Gooseberry agreed.

So Gary Gooseberry and Adam Artichoke set off to Terry Turnip's house to ask him to help too.

'Hello! I'm sorry I hurt you today.' said Gary Gooseberry. 'Please can you help me with a special surprise for my mum?'

'Yes I will, but only if you promise to always be nice to me.' said Terry Turnip.

Gary Gooseberry agreed.

So Gary Gooseberry, Adam Artichoke and Terry Turnip set off to Monty Marrow's house to ask him to help too.

'Hello! Please will you help me with a special surprise for my mum?' asked Gary Gooseberry.

'Yes I will, but only if you promise to always be nice to me.' said Monty Marrow.

Gary Gooseberry agreed.

So Gary Gooseberry, Adam Artichoke, Terry Turnip and Monty Marrow set off back to Gary Gooseberry's house.

On the way they saw Lee Lemon swinging on the tree swing.

'Where are you all going to?' asked Lee Lemon.

'They are helping me to decorate my house as a surprise for my mummy.' said Gary Gooseberry.

'Can I help too?' enquired Lee Lemon.

'Of course you can, the more the merrier.' said Monty Marrow.

When they reached Gary Gooseberry's house, Mrs Gooseberry had gone shopping.

She had taken most of his brother's and sister's with her, but the two who were left at home agreed to help too.

They quickly set to work.

Adam Artichoke and Lee Lemon painted the roof red.

Monty Marrow cut back the bushes.

Terry Turnip mowed the lawn.

Gary Gooseberry painted the front of the house white and his brother's painted the doors and windows in bright red paint, to match the roof.

Soon, with everybody helping, the house was finished and gleaming. It looked like a whole new house.

Not long after, Mrs. Gooseberry returned home from the shops.

At first, she thought she had gone to the wrong house. She could not believe her eyes.

Mrs. Gooseberry was very, very happy.

Gary Gooseberry apologised to his mum and YumYum friends for being naughty and thanked them all for helping.

Mrs. Gooseberry thanked them all for their hard work, with a glass of delicious chocolate mudshake and gave Gary Gooseberry and his two brothers an extra big hug and kiss on the cheek.

Nowadays, the house still looks like new and Gary Gooseberry is still being nice.

The End...........but just before you go....

Remember to eat your 5-a-day !!

Gary Gooseberry is low in Saturated Fat, Cholesterol and Sodium. High in Dietary Fibre, Vitamin C, Vitamin A, Potassium and Manganese.

Using this story write the names of the 5 main characters on a piece of paper, and then visit **www.5adayworld.co.uk/theyumyums** for lots of fun and games as well as more information on your daily portions and tasty recipe ideas.
The Recommended Daily Portion for each of your 5 fruit and vegetables is 80g.
Fresh is best, but canned and frozen still counts towards your allowance.
The YumYums top tip for staying healthy is 'Grab a Smoothie!'

Merchandise Offer

Let the 5-a-day YumYums protect your bedroom, with these colourful door hangers. We will also send you a YumYums club membership number and regular updates, as to what is happening in 5-a-day world.

Ask an adult to cut out this page and send it with a 50p coin, including your choice of character and eagerly await your door hanger. Whilst you're waiting visit our website www.5dayworld.co.uk or email enquiries@5adayworld.co.uk, to let us know who your favourite character is:

You can choose from:-

Pink   **Blue**

Trisha Tomato   Barry Banana
Sally Strawberry   Martin Mushroom
Belinda Beetroot   Olly Onion
Polly Peach   William Watermelon
Chloe Cucumber   Gary Gooseberry

*Illustration purposes only

To be completed by an adult:

Please rush me my choice of Door Hanger below as below and make me a member of 'The YumYum's' club.

I enclose 1 Voucher and a 50p.
(only 1 door hanger per application)

Child's Name: _____

Age: _____

Attach coin here

Choice of Character: _____

Address: _____

_____

Parents Name : _____

Parents Signature: _____

Where did you purchase this book? Bookshop / supermarket / newsagent
/ given as gift (please circle)
Other: _____

Send your request to:-
Di-Med Publishing Ltd, P O BOX 93, Brighouse, West Yorkshire HD6 9AA.
*Delivery within 28 days. Subject to availability. If your choice of character is unavailable an alternative will be sent as a substitute. Proof of postage, is not proof of receipt. Your details will not be passed onto any other party, other than those within 5-a-day world.